CRAZY
HORSE

SIOUX WARRIOR

SPECIAL LIVES IN HISTORY THAT BECOME

Signature LIVES

CRAZY
HORSE
SIOUX WARRIOR

By Brenda Haugen

Content Adviser: Dr. Jerry C. Bread, Outreach Coordinator,
Native American Studies Department,
University of Oklahoma, Tulsa

Reading Adviser: Rosemary G. Palmer, Ph.D.,
Department of Literacy, College of Education,
Boise State University

COMPASS POINT BOOKS MINNEAPOLIS, MINNESOTA

Compass Point Books
3109 West 50th Street, #115
Minneapolis, MN 55410

Visit Compass Point Books on the Internet at *www.compasspointbooks.com*
or e-mail your request to *custserv@compasspointbooks.com*

To Nicole—BLH

Editor: Editorial Directions, Inc.
Lead Designer: Jaime Martens
Photo Researcher: Marcie C. Spence
Page Production: The Design Lab, Bobbie Nuytten
Cartographer: XNR Productions, Inc.
Educational Consultant: Diane Smolinski

Managing Editor: Catherine Neitge
Creative Director: Keith Griffin
Editorial Director: Carol Jones

Library of Congress Cataloging-in-Publication Data
Haugen, Brenda.
  Crazy Horse : Sioux warrior / by Brenda Haugen.
    p. cm.— (Signature lives)
  Includes bibliographical references and index.
  ISBN 0-7565-0999-8 (hardcover)
  1. Crazy Horse, ca. 1842–1877. 2. Oglala Indians—Kings and rulers—
Biography. 3. Oglala Indians—Government relations. 4. Oglala Indians—
Wars. 5. Little Bighorn, Battle of the, Mont., 1876. I. Title. II. Series.
  E99.O3C72345 2006
  978.004'975244'0092—dc22   2005003257

Signature Lives

AMERICAN FRONTIER ERA

By the late 1700s, the United States was growing into a nation of homesteaders, politicians, mountain men, and American dreams. Manifest Destiny propelled settlers to push west, conquering and "civilizing" from coast to coast. In keeping with this vision, world leaders hammered out historic agreements such as the Louisiana Purchase, which drastically increased U.S. territory. This ambition often led to bitter conflicts with Native Americans trying to protect their way of life and their traditional lands. Life on the frontier was often filled with danger and difficulties. The people who wove their way into American history overcame these challenges with a courage and conviction that defined an era and shaped a nation.

Table of Contents

Chapter
1 A HERO FOR HIS PEOPLE

ⅇↄⲅↃꙬↄ

With a heavy heart, Crazy Horse led his people where he hoped he'd never go—to the white soldiers at Fort Robinson, Nebraska.

Crazy Horse hated what these settlers had done to his land and people. But he realized his only choice was to turn to them for help.

The winter of 1876–77 had proved particularly brutal. Day after day, temperatures dipped way below the freezing point. Crazy Horse and his people were freezing from the cold and suffering from the lack of food. Wild game proved increasingly difficult to find as white settlers heading west chased the animals away. The 35-year-old Oglala Sioux warrior was worried.

So in May 1877, Crazy Horse brought 900 Oglala

Crazy Horse was both an Indian warrior and a hero to his people, the Oglala Sioux.

Sioux to Fort Robinson. Crazy Horse would have preferred to roam the Great Plains as a loner, free to hunt and fight as needed. But his decisions and actions affected countless others who depended on him.

Crazy Horse had a reputation for taking care of others. He always made sure that his tribe didn't go hungry. Crazy Horse became a great warrior, but he never looked for attention or bragged about his actions.

Crazy Horse felt he had no choice but to bring his people to Fort Robinson.

In this and other ways, Crazy Horse was different from those around him. He even looked differ-

ent. According to Short Buffalo, a Sioux who knew Crazy Horse, he was:

" not very tall and not very short, neither broad nor thin. His hair was very light. Crazy Horse had a very light complexion, much lighter than other Indians. His face was not broad, and he had a high, sharp nose. He had black eyes that hardly ever looked straight at a man, but they didn't miss much that was going on, all the same."

More likely to listen than to speak, Crazy Horse became part of the Sioux's inner circle of decision-making when he was a child. Because he kept quiet, he often got to listen in on adult conversations. Others trusted him not to reveal anything that was said in confidence.

As Crazy Horse grew older, he attended Sioux councils where tribal leaders made plans for the future. Even then, he usually sat quietly, listening and observing all around him.

The Sioux Indians were divided into three different tribes: the Dakota, Nakota, and Lakota. Each tribe was divided into bands, or groups of related people. The Mdewakanton, Wahpekute, Sisseton, and Wahpeton made up the Dakota who lived in present-day Minnesota and eastern North and South Dakota. The Nakota included the Yankton and Yanktonai who lived in eastern North and South Dakota. The largest of the three tribes, the Lakota, lived west of the Missouri River in North and South Dakota, Wyoming, and Montana. This western tribe, sometimes called the Teton, was made up of seven bands, including Crazy Horse's band, the Oglala.

Crazy Horse often attended Sioux councils.

But as quiet as he often was, no one was bolder or braver than Crazy Horse on the battlefield. He proved his courage in raids against his tribe's enemies and in important battles such as the Little Bighorn.

Crazy Horse became a symbol of Sioux courage, dignity, and freedom. He clung to the Sioux way of life for as long as he could, fighting restrictions on where and when his people could hunt. A loner at heart, he enjoyed roaming the prairie, and he rebelled against being told where to live.

Throughout his life, Crazy Horse saw white

settlers moving onto land the Sioux had loved and respected for generations. He remembered the days when the grasslands were filled with buffalo for as far as the eye could see. As more and more settlers moved west, they destroyed entire areas of grasslands and nearly wiped out the buffalo. As the buffalo died, the Sioux way of life began to die as well.

Not long after bringing his people to Fort Robinson, Crazy Horse met an early end. With the death of Crazy Horse, the Sioux fight for freedom died, too. ✍

2 A Boy Named Curly

❧❧❧

Right from the start, everyone knew this baby boy was different from other children in the Oglala Sioux tribe. His skin looked lighter, and his head was topped with wavy, light brown hair. Years before he earned the name Crazy Horse, the future Sioux warrior was called Curly.

The Sioux didn't keep records, so no one is sure of the exact date of Curly's birth. Historians believe he was born sometime in 1840 at a favorite Sioux gathering place by the Belle Fourche River. This river ran near Bear Butte in present-day Sturgis, South Dakota.

Curly was welcomed into the world by an older sister and parents named Crazy Horse and Rattle Blanket Woman. Another son called Little Hawk completed the young family. Rattle Blanket Woman died young, and Crazy Horse married her sister, who helped raise his three children.

Curly grew up listening to warriors tell exciting tales of buffalo hunts and war parties. He played catch with his friends, using a ball filled with antelope hair. They also shot arrows at tree stumps or buffalo chips. The boy whose arrow landed closest to the target was declared the winner. Curly also loved to swim.

> *Warriors usually didn't get their permanent names until they grew up and earned them in battle or through other deeds.*

Along with playing games, Curly enjoyed caring for the tribe's horses. Even as a young boy, he proved he had a way with horses. Not only was he adept at catching and taming them, he was also good at taking them from other tribes. Because of this skill, he earned the name His Horses Looking, although most people still called him Curly.

Though he rarely boasted about his accomplishments, Curly enjoyed participating in friendly competition. He and his friends raced their ponies and competed to see who was best at handling bows and arrows.

Curly came from a humble family. His father was a holy man who interpreted dreams for his people. They didn't own many horses or other belongings,

Young Curly enjoyed playing games with other members of his tribe.

but Curly's family was content. They had enough food to eat and the freedom to travel as they wished, visiting friends and relatives in other tribes.

Curly spent much of his childhood near the Holy Road, known to white people as the Oregon Trail. This road cut through the heart of the buffalo herds that filled the central Plains during Curly's youth.

Curly and Little Hawk and their friends Hump and Lone Bear often pestered the pioneers heading west on the Holy Road. Gold had been discovered in California in 1848. This event drew a steady stream of people from the East who planned to find their

Travelers along the Oregon Trail during the 1800s

fortunes in the West. Sometimes the boys got travelers to share sugar, coffee, and other goods with them. Occasionally, the youngsters would simply steal what they wanted.

Travelers on the Holy Road often expressed surprise at Curly's appearance. When they noticed his light coloring, they doubted that he was even an Indian! They suspected he had been captured by the

Sioux and raised among them. Curly hated being called a captive. He was just as much a Sioux as his friends were.

Though he liked the treats he got from the travelers, Curly would have preferred that they stop moving onto his people's land. The prairie sported few trees, but those that stood were quickly cut down and used as firewood. Pioneers' wagons tore up the grasslands, and their cattle and horses ate up all the greenery. This destruction of the environment chased buffalo and other game away. Many of the animals that stayed were killed by travelers' guns.

The white settlers weren't going away, though. They believed in Manifest Destiny—the idea that the United States was destined to stretch all the way across North America, from the Atlantic Ocean to the Pacific.

The U.S. government helped the settlers on their journey along the Holy Road. About 100 soldiers were stationed at Fort Laramie, Wyoming. These

The Sioux were a nomadic people who followed their lifeline— the buffalo. The animals were the Indians' main source of food but also provided the Sioux with clothing, shelter, tools, and other necessities of life. In 1850, about 20 million buffalo roamed the Plains of the United States. By 1889, only about 1,000 remained. These huge creatures measured 6 feet (1.8 meters) tall at the humps on their backs and weighed more than 2,000 pounds (907 kilograms). They ate grasses that grew on the Plains.

The U.S. government stationed troops at Fort Laramie, Wyoming.

soldiers were ordered to protect citizens from Indians who would beg or steal from them.

The Horse Creek Treaty of 1851 was supposed to end these problems. In exchange for not bothering travelers anymore, the Plains Indians who agreed to the treaty would be given supplies each year. The treaty was not a success. U.S. soldiers didn't realize that the Indian leaders who agreed to it really had no authority to make decisions for their people. Now they insisted that one chief be chosen as the Indians' leader. A Brulé Sioux named Conquering Bear was selected. The whites didn't understand that chiefs were respected within their tribes but didn't rule like a governor or a president would.

Conquering Bear agreed to let U.S. citizens use the Holy Road in peace. In exchange, Sioux tribes would receive $50,000 in goods each year. But Conquering Bear held no authority over the rest of the Sioux. If they chose to ignore the agreement, he couldn't stop them. Conquering Bear knew it, and so did the other Indians. Unfortunately, white soldiers were not aware of this fact.

These misunderstandings caused confusion and frustration for both Indians and whites. Instead of ending conflict, the treaty started even greater hostility between the two groups. Soon a frightened cow, an angry traveler, and a camp of Indians would come together to create an explosive situation, and nothing would ever be the same. ⊱

Chapter

3 THE MORMON COW

Curly opened his eyes to see his father standing above him. He could tell right away that Crazy Horse was angry.

Curly had wandered off alone into territory frequented by Sioux enemies—the Pawnee and the Crow. To make matters worse, Curly disappeared shortly after trouble had come to the Sioux camp. Crazy Horse had been beside himself with worry.

On August 17, 1854, a stray cow caused havoc in a Sioux camp near Fort Laramie. As Indian children followed behind her, whooping and hollering, the animal ran through a Sioux family's lodge. By the time she emerged on the other side, some of their belongings had become tangled on her horns.

The cow's owner, a Mormon pioneer traveling on

As white pio-neers headed West, the Sioux were often forced to fight to preserve their lands.

the Holy Road, ran after her but immediately stopped when he reached the edge of the Sioux camp. Suddenly, a gunshot rang out. A warrior named High Forehead had killed the cow.

Scared and angry, the man ran back to his wagon as the Sioux people laughed. But the incident ultimately proved to be no laughing matter. The traveler headed to Fort Laramie, where Lieutenant Hugh Fleming heard his complaint.

Meanwhile, the Indians didn't let the cow go to waste. Although the meat proved too tough to be tasty, they still used the hide. In fact, Curly fashioned two war clubs from it—one for himself and one for his friend He Dog. He took the cow hide and bound together the clubs' handles and their stone heads.

The weapons worked well but didn't mean as much to Curly as his first club had. His friend Hump had made a war club for him out of the first buffalo Curly had killed. Awhile back, another Indian boy named Pretty One had taken the special club from Curly's belt and thrown it into the Laramie River. Curly desperately tried to find the club in the water, but it was gone. The incident proved to be one of the many times Pretty One would hurt Curly.

At the fort, the cow's owner and the white soldiers discussed what should be done. Lieutenant Fleming sent for Conquering Bear. Neither man wanted any more trouble. At first, they both laughed about the incident, but the situation quickly got out of hand, thanks to an interpreter named Wyuse. The son of a trader, Wyuse was married to a Lakota Sioux woman. But even though he had ties to the Indians, he sometimes twisted their words when interpreting for them. This is what happened at the meeting between Conquering Bear and Lieutenant Fleming. Soon, the lieutenant stopped laughing and turned red in anger.

An interpreter (back row, left) poses with a group of Native Americans. Interpreters had the power to either strengthen or destroy relations between whites and Indians.

Trying to calm Lieutenant Fleming, Conquering Bear offered the Mormon the pick of his best horses. Lieutenant Fleming refused and called for High Forehead's surrender. Conquering Bear tried to explain he had no authority to arrest High Forehead. Conquering Bear was a Brulé, and High Forehead was a Miniconjou.

Another lieutenant at Fort Laramie, John Grattan, volunteered to capture High Forehead. Grattan took 31 soldiers and the interpreter Wyuse and headed for the Sioux camp.

Curly quietly watched the scene from the riverbank with his friend Young Bear. Conquering Bear made one last attempt to settle the argument peacefully. He agreed to give up five horses, but Grattan only desired High Forehead's arrest. High Forehead didn't want to cause trouble for the other Sioux, but he didn't want to be arrested either.

"I am alone now," he told the other Sioux. "Last fall the whites killed my two brothers. This spring my uncle, my only relative, died. Today my hands are full of weapons, my arms strong. I will not go alive."

Wyuse lied when he translated High Forehead's words for the soldiers. He led them to believe that the other Sioux refused to surrender High Forehead.

Lieutenant Grattan grew angry. Still, Conquering Bear tried to keep the situation under control. He said he would turn High Forehead over to the soldiers. Again, Wyuse told the troops a different story. Lieutenant Grattan finally lost his patience. His soldiers readied their weapons and fired, killing Conquering Bear's brother.

Lieutenant Grattan ordered his men to continue firing. Cannon blasts tore up Sioux lodges. Then a shot hit Conquering Bear. As their beloved chief fell

Conquering Bear was mortally wounded during the conflict between Grattan and the Sioux.

to the ground, the Sioux attacked the soldiers. High Forehead shot Lieutenant Grattan.

Nearly 1,200 Indian warriors had been watching the discussions from where Curly was hiding. When the fighting started, Curly's uncle Spotted Tail led them from the riverbank. Hundreds of arrows flew from the warriors' bows, and soon all the soldiers and the interpreter lay dead.

Conquering Bear was mortally wounded, but he struggled against death. Curly heard Conquering Bear's wife crying in their lodge. As Hump went inside to care for Conquering Bear, Curly peeked in and saw the dying chief. Conquering Bear's skin looked pale, and his eyes were empty.

The sight brought sadness to Curly's heart. He ran to his horse and rode to the bluffs to be alone. He searched for direction in his life. He hoped to have a vision, or dream, that would tell him what to do.

Curly stayed in the bluffs for three days before his father and Hump found him. Curly explained why he went to the bluffs, but his explanation only made Crazy Horse and Hump angrier. The Sioux believed people had to prepare for visions. Curly should have talked with the tribe's wise men and asked for guidance or gone to a sweat lodge with his father to purify himself. The very least he should have done was tell someone where he was going.

The Grattan Massacre marked the start of what have been called the Sioux Wars. Battles between whites and Indians would rage on until 1890.

After seeing their anger, Curly decided that now wasn't the time to tell them what he had dreamed. While it didn't seem like much of a vision at the time, it would shape the rest of his life—and warn him about his own death.

4 REVENGE

⚬⚭⚬

As a teenager, Curly joined other Plains Indians in harassing travelers along the Holy Road. The Indians clung to the hope that whites might eventually give up and quit heading west. But nothing the Indians did stopped them from coming.

News of the Grattan Massacre brought thoughts of revenge to many soldiers. Between their anger and the Indians' wish that the whites would go away, peace didn't look possible.

In August 1855, the U.S. government took action. It sent officials to tell the Sioux they must come to Fort Laramie. If they followed this order, the Sioux were promised protection. Those ignoring the order would be considered hostile enemies of the United States.

Even though Curly and other Sioux wished otherwise, white settlers continued heading west along the Holy Road.

More than half the Sioux came to Fort Laramie, setting up their homes nearby. About 700 Sioux households already lived near the fort. Now another 400 families joined them.

The Sioux that ignored U.S. government orders were hunted by soldiers who were eager to avenge the lives lost in the Grattan Massacre. At Fort Kearny in the Nebraska Territory, General William S. Harney gathered about 600 soldiers. Harney heard that a Brulé Indian named Little Thunder and his people refused to go to Fort Laramie. As General Harney headed toward Fort Laramie with his men, he

The U.S. government ordered the Sioux to move to Fort Laramie.

discovered Little Thunder's village tucked along the Bluewater River, just north of the soldiers' route.

Harney went to the village and talked with Little Thunder, Spotted Tail, and another Sioux chief named Iron Shell. Having just returned from a successful buffalo hunt, the camp buzzed with activity. The men put away their weapons while the women cleaned the buffalo hides. As Harney talked outside the village with the three unarmed leaders, his troops circled the village unnoticed. Harney had planned all along to attack the Indians.

Fort Laramie started out as a trading post. In 1834, Cheyenne and Arapaho Indians traded their furs there. When the gold rush began in the late 1840s, the fort became a place where white travelers could buy supplies on their way to the West.

Harney's troops tore through the village and killed 86 people. The attack only lasted a few minutes but proved to be a massacre.

Curly had been visiting the Brulé village but wasn't there during the attack. He and four of his Brulé friends had gone out hunting. When they returned to Little Thunder's village on September 3, 1855, they saw only smoldering wreckage. While his friends disappeared to avoid further danger, young Curly felt a responsibility to stay and help.

Curly carefully searched the area and found two survivors—a Cheyenne named Yellow Woman, who had been visiting the Brulés, and her newborn baby. Yellow Woman had gone into labor during the attack. Soldiers had killed the rest of her family.

Taking Yellow Woman and her baby to safety, Curly stumbled upon other survivors. He learned that Little Thunder and Spotted Tail suffered injuries in the battle and that many others had been captured.

Curly took Yellow Woman and her baby back to her Cheyenne camp in Kansas. For saving their lives, Curly was seen as a hero. The Cheyenne tribe considered him a friend.

The massacre at the Brulé village taught the Sioux many things. They realized their bows and

General William S. Harney

arrows, tomahawks, clubs, and other weapons were no match for the guns and cannons of the soldiers. They also understood that, with these weapons, the soldiers could destroy their villages anytime they wanted.

Battered and tired of fighting, three Sioux leaders—Spotted Tail, Red Leaf, and Long Chin —chose to surrender. They reported to Fort Laramie.

Shortly after they arrived, the three leaders were sent to jail at Fort Kearny. The U.S. government was punishing them for their part in the robbery of a mail coach and the deaths of the three men accompanying it. The chiefs had attacked the coach in November 1854 to avenge the death of Conquering Bear. Long Chin and Red Leaf were Conquering Bear's brothers, and Spotted Tail was his nephew.

U.S. soldiers jailed Spotted Tail at Fort Kearny.

Curly felt his anger rise as Spotted Tail was led away with Long Chin and Red Leaf. Many innocent people had been killed by both Indians and whites. When the Sioux leaders surrendered, they were jailed. Where was the justice for the deaths of the innocent Sioux? The more he saw of the white man's behavior, the more Curly believed in what his warrior friend Hump told him: It was better to die fighting than to be imprisoned by whites.

5 CURLY BECOMES CRAZY HORSE

⌁⌁⌁

After spending nearly a year visiting friends and relatives and enjoying time alone, Curly showed up for a big meeting of the Sioux in August 1857. More than 5,000 Sioux were present at Bear Butte, just north of their holy land—the Black Hills. They needed to discuss the problems between their tribe and white settlers. The settlers were ruining Indian hunting grounds with their wagons and livestock and were chasing buffalo and other wild game away. Something needed to be done before the hunting grounds and the Indians' way of life were destroyed.

As the meeting drew to a close, not much had been decided. They had feasted, danced, and enjoyed one another's company, but the Indians still didn't know what to do about white people moving

During the 1800s, white settlers nearly wiped out the buffalo, which was a primary source of food for the Sioux and other tribes.

through their land. But Curly, who was nearly 16, had made a decision. It was time to tell his father about the vision he'd had about three years earlier.

Crazy Horse and Curly fasted and built a sweat lodge. The lodge's shell was made of buffalo skins spread across poles built from willow tree branches. In the center of the lodge, father and son dug a shallow pit. After heating rocks in a fire, they put the stones in the pit. They threw cold water on the stones to create steam to make them sweat. Crazy Horse and Curly entered the lodge to purify themselves. As they sweated, Curly told his father about his vision and asked him what he thought it meant.

In his vision, Curly saw a lone horseman dressed in blue leggings and a white deerskin shirt. The man wore no war paint and had a single feather in his flowing brown hair. A small brown stone was tied behind his ear. The horseman told Curly to dress the same way and ordered him not to wear paint or other decorations. He said Curly should throw dust over himself and his horse before going into battle. The horseman appeared to float above the ground. Bullets and arrows flew around him, but he remained uninjured.

> *The Black Hills span about 6,000 square miles (15,600 square kilometers) of land in present-day southwestern South Dakota and eastern Wyoming. A range of low, beautiful mountains, they reach up to 4,000 feet (1,220 km) above the terrain.*

The horseman warned Curly to never keep anything for himself.

When building sweat lodges, Plains Indians used branches to create the structures' shells.

After Curly finished his story, his father was silent for quite a while. Finally, he spoke.

"The man on the horse is what you must become—did you not see his hair, how bright and long—or how he thought?"

Curly realized his father spoke the truth. Curly knew what the man in his vision was thinking. The only way that was possible was if the man represented Curly himself.

Crazy Horse told Curly to dress as the horseman had instructed. He explained that when the horseman ordered Curly to keep nothing for himself, he meant that Curly should share food and other items with the poor and helpless in his tribe.

In another part of the vision, Curly saw the horseman's own people holding back the man's arms. Crazy Horse interpreted this to mean that Curly could only be injured if his arms were held back by the Sioux.

While waiting for his vision, Curly went without food and water, and he stayed awake for nearly three days. His tongue thick with thirst and his eyes aching, Curly lay on the hard ground. He wanted to be as uncomfortable as possible so he wouldn't fall asleep.

Old enough to be a warrior, Curly almost always lived by the lessons he'd learned from his vision. When he forgot what he'd been told, he paid the price.

In the summer of 1858, Curly got the chance to prove his bravery in a battle against the Arapaho. Curly's friend Hump led the Sioux warriors in a fight to take the Arapaho's horses.

Like the man in his vision, Curly was unharmed by flying arrows as he charged at Arapaho warriors. He slipped up, though, when two warriors rode out to challenge him. Curly killed them both

and took their scalps, forgetting the horseman's warning to not take anything for himself. As Curly collected the scalps, an arrow pierced his leg.

Quickly realizing his mistake, Curly threw the scalps away and hobbled back to safety. Hump cut the arrow from Curly's leg and bandaged the wound.

The battle raged on for about two hours. Hump's men killed four Arapaho warriors and suffered no

In 1858, Curly and other Sioux led a raid to steal horses from the Arapaho.

41

losses. The Sioux had managed to win some fine horses from their enemy. Successful in their efforts, Curly and the other warriors headed home.

A big victory dance was held in camp that night, but Curly stayed in the shadows. As other warriors talked about their brave acts in battle, Curly kept quiet. Twice his warrior friends pushed him into the circle to share his battle stories, but both times he

Curly, Hump, and other Sioux were victorious in their battle with the Arapaho.

held his tongue. Others would have to tell Curly's tales—and they did.

The battle reinforced Curly's belief in his vision. What the horseman told him had proved true. The fighting also gave Curly a chance to demonstrate his courage, which he did. When Crazy Horse learned of his son's bravery, Curly earned something very important—a new name. His father took the name Worm and gave his son the name Crazy Horse. ॐ

Chapter

6 BLACK BUFFALO WOMAN

⤶⧓⤷

As a young warrior, Crazy Horse continued to prove himself in battle, but he always remained generous. The horses he captured over the years would have made a fine herd, but he saved only the animals he needed—one or two good hunting horses and two or three to ride into battle. He gave the rest to other members of his tribe.

His modesty never changed either. Others gladly shared their stories of bravery on the battlefield. By telling their tales, they hoped to earn honor and advance to higher positions in the tribe. To Crazy Horse, that wasn't important.

Unfortunately, Crazy Horse's lack of wealth proved to be a problem in one area of his life: earning the affections of a certain woman.

Unlike many of his fellow warriors, Crazy Horse was modest and never boasted of his deeds in battle.

When he was younger, he teased a pretty little girl as she picked wild plums with the women. He'd toss stones at her to get her attention but was embarrassed when the women noticed him. He saw her again at the gathering in 1857. She caught Crazy Horse looking at her on more than one occasion. In time, they would become less shy around each other.

By 1861, Crazy Horse realized he had fallen in love with Black Buffalo Woman—but he wasn't the only one. Others with more horses and more important relatives waited in line to share a few moments of conversation with the beautiful young woman.

One warrior ranked so high in importance that he didn't even have to wait in line. No Water owned many horses and came from a respected family. If he wanted to talk with Black Buffalo Woman, he pushed his way to the front. Others didn't like it, but they couldn't protest.

But Black Buffalo Woman seemed more interested in Crazy Horse. As was the custom, Crazy Horse pulled his blanket around himself and Black Buffalo Woman so they could talk privately. At times, an old woman who lived in Black Buffalo Woman's lodge tore the blanket away so Crazy Horse would leave and give other warriors a chance to talk with the girl. Crazy Horse was embarrassed by this, but it didn't stop him from being with her as much as possible. Even the other warriors teased

A Native American plays his flute for young women outside their teepee.

him about taking more of the girl's time than he deserved.

"Let us rescue the Lakota captive in the blanket of Crazy Horse!" they'd playfully cry.

Crazy Horse watched Black Buffalo Woman dance and play games with friends. He decided he would have to start building a home that would prove comfortable for her and agreeable to her family.

The year 1861 was a good one for the Oglala Sioux. Hunting was good, and food was plentiful even throughout the winter. More whites traveled the Holy Road in search of gold, and telegraph wires now found their way across Sioux territory. The soldiers, however, were too busy to bother the Indians much. The Civil War had broken out, and U.S. troops left to fight in the eastern part of the United States.

In the summer of 1862, the Sioux continued to fight their Indian enemies. Red Cloud, his brothers No Water and Black Twin, and Hump and his warriors prepared to battle the Crow. Worm watched with pride as both his sons—Crazy Horse and Little

By 1861, the Civil War drew U.S. soldiers back East. This bloody conflict lasted from 1861 until 1865.

Hawk—got ready to ride off with the war party.

As the Sioux gathered to leave, No Water complained of a toothache. The Sioux took it as a warning that he shouldn't head into battle, so No Water stayed behind.

Two weeks later, Red Cloud and his men returned victorious. They'd attacked a Crow village and had driven members of that tribe away. Little Hawk had been hurt in the fighting, but Crazy Horse dragged him to safety. No one was ever worried about being left behind if Crazy Horse was along. He often risked his own life to ensure the safety of others.

But before the triumphant Sioux reached their village, Crazy Horse was greeted by Woman's Dress—the man who had been called Pretty One as a child. He had news that filled Crazy Horse with sorrow.

"Someone has been walking under the blanket," Woman's Dress said. He meant that someone had gotten married.

Starting in the 1840s, people used the telegraph to send messages. Operators passed messages with instruments that interrupted electric flow along a wire. The length of the bursts of current and the spaces between them stood for letters in Morse code. Translators on the other end of the message interpreted the clicks made by their machines and wrote out the information being sent.

While the telegraph made life easier for some, the Indians didn't appreciate countless wires and poles cutting across their land. They also feared that the new invention would scare the buffalo away.

Red Cloud may have arranged the marriage between No Water and Black Buffalo Woman.

While the war party was away, No Water married Black Buffalo Woman. Many believed Red Cloud had arranged the marriage by planning the war party and having No Water fake a toothache so he could stay behind. Black Buffalo Woman was Red Cloud's niece. Red Cloud strengthened his own position by arranging her marriage into an important family.

But the reasons didn't matter to Crazy Horse. His heart was broken. After hearing the news, Crazy Horse went to his parents' lodge and wrapped himself in his sleeping robes. His family left him alone to deal with his sadness. His father placed pieces of brush in front of the lodge. This signaled that no one was home. He knew Crazy Horse wanted to be by himself.

After a few days of grieving, Crazy Horse got out of bed and left to take his anger out on the Crow. He told no one about his travels, but he did come back with a gun (which he gave to Little Hawk), a pair of glasses that had probably been worn by a white officer, and two Crow scalps, which he threw to the dogs. Then Crazy Horse went to the sweat lodge. Afterward, he seemed like his old self.

A while later, Crazy Horse spotted Black Buffalo Woman picking herbs as he returned home from a hunt. When she saw him, she quickly threw her blanket over her face. Crazy Horse rode toward her. When he didn't say anything mean or angry, she lowered the blanket. Looking at the ground, she said, "I had my duty to my father and brothers."

A respected Oglala Sioux chief, Red Cloud (1822–1909) became an important mediator between the U.S. government and the Native Americans.

Crazy Horse wasn't happy, but he understood. "I would have everything good between us," he said. "I have made a vow that it should be so. There can be no anger in my heart, even against myself."

Crazy Horse rode away, but it wouldn't be their last encounter. ❧

Chapter

7 A SHIRT-WEARER

❧⌘❧

As more white people traveled the Holy Road, buffalo and other wild game became scarce. A great herd of buffalo once covered the Plains, but traffic on the Holy Road had broken the herd into two smaller groups, one to the north of the road and the other to the south.

Whites hunted the buffalo for sport and profit, as well. They eventually drove the animal close to extinction. They didn't use the whole buffalo like the Indians did. Often, white hunters only wanted the hides, which would fetch a good price back East. The meat was left behind to rot or be eaten by wolves.

In an effort to stop traffic on the Holy Road once and for all, about 1,000 Sioux warriors—including Crazy Horse—attacked settlers at a crossing on the

Unlike white hunters, Indians who killed the buffalo typically made use of the entire animal.

In 1865, the Sioux attacked settlers along the North Platte River.

North Platte River. They launched the attack on July 25, 1865.

Crazy Horse served as one of about 20 decoys who tried to lure the soldiers guarding the bridge out of their protected spot. But before the soldiers had a chance to fall for the trap, the warriors who were hiding lost patience, broke their cover, and became clearly visible to the soldiers. Knowing they were about to be attacked, the soldiers refused to pay any heed to the decoys. Crazy Horse was enraged, but there was nothing he could do. The next day, the Indian warriors went home in defeat.

Because the Sioux depended on the buffalo to survive, they had to follow the animals wherever they roamed. As time went on, this brought them into enemy territory—lands belonging to the Crow, Shoshone, Pawnee, and others. Naturally, these Indians wouldn't let the Sioux travel freely on their lands, and more and more fighting erupted among the tribes.

Another change was occurring within the Sioux community. Through the years, many Indians had become accustomed to white trading posts and forts near their camps. Sometimes Indians would trade hides for sugar, coffee, and other items. Crazy Horse didn't like what this trade was doing to his people. They were losing skills they'd passed down for generations. They were forgetting how to make tools because it was easier to trade for them. And they longed for foods they'd never known before and had once been quite happy without.

Others in Crazy Horse's tribe also felt it was time to return to the old ways. These Indians began rebuilding old traditions. One was the custom of naming shirt-wearers for the tribe.

Shirt-wearers were leaders who served as role models for everyone else. They were chosen for their courage and generosity and were required to put their selfishness aside and to always think of the

As trade increased between Native Americans and white settlers, many Indians lost touch with their traditional way of life.

tribe's welfare first. The Sioux elders met to pick four shirt-wearers.

The air felt electric as everyone gathered for the special ceremony. A group of men who assisted the elders circled the camp on horses, stopping four times to choose the shirt-wearers. The first picked was Young Man Afraid, the son of Old Man Afraid—a great leader among the Sioux. The second was Sword, the son of Chief Brave Bear. American Horse, the son of another leader—Sitting Bear—was named the third shirt-wearer.

Crazy Horse stood with the others, waiting to see who'd be the final man honored. A noise of happy exclamation rippled through those gathered as the Sioux riders stopped by Crazy Horse. Woman's Dress had been standing nearby. He had expected to be chosen and so was wearing a new deerskin for the occasion. Woman's Dress was the first to leave the celebration that followed, and he walked away angry.

Old Man Afraid had been made the new chief by Conquering Bear as he was dying in 1854. Old Man Afraid considered Crazy Horse's father one of his close friends and often came to him for advice.

The four shirt-wearers were carried to the center of the council lodge, where they were seated on fine robes. Elders and leaders sat on one side of the lodge, and warriors and their fathers sat on the other. Women and children filled in the other two sides.

There was a great feast that included buffalo and other wild game. After the meal, the elders explained the shirt-wearers' duties. They were to lead warriors both inside and outside the camp. They were to ensure that all people's rights were respected. They also were responsible for keeping peace in the camp at all times.

The four chosen men were given beautiful shirts made from the skins of bighorn sheep. Each man also received a single eagle feather to wear flat on

A traditional
Sioux warrior's
shirt

the back of his head. Then one of the elders spoke:

> Wear the shirts, my sons, and be big-
> hearted men, always helping others, never
> thinking of yourselves. Look out for the
> poor, the widows and orphans and all
> those of little power; help them. Think no
> ill of others nor see the ill they would do to
> you. Many dogs may come to lift the leg at
> your lodge, but look the other way, and do
> not let your heart carry the remembering.
> Do not give way to anger, even if relatives
> lie in blood before you. I know these

things are hard to do, my sons, but we have chosen you as great-hearted. Do all these duties gladly, and with a good face. Be generous and strong and brave in them, and if for all these things an enemy comes against you, go boldly forward, for it is better to lie a naked warrior in death than to be wrapped up well with a heart of water inside.

The personalities of the four warriors were reflected in their reactions to the great honor they had just received. Pride shone on the face of American Horse as he drank in all the glory. Young Man Afraid took everything in stride. While he was pleased to be chosen, he was used to being honored as part of an important family. Sword's face glowed with appreciation at being among the chosen few.

As usual, Crazy Horse appeared embarrassed by all the attention. He sat quietly, looking straight ahead. But many eyes fell upon him—including those of Black Buffalo Woman. She stood at the celebration with one son at her side and one on her back. Some whispered that she had chosen the wrong husband. Perhaps she was thinking the same thing.

The shirt-wearers' sleeves sported fringes of hair. Each lock represented a deed done in battle, such as a wound received, a scalp taken, or a horse captured. More than 240 locks of hair hung from Crazy Horse's shirt.

Chapter

8

MORE BATTLES
IN THE QUEST
FOR GOLD

∿

In 1866, gold was discovered in Montana. It didn't take long before the soldiers realized they'd need a safe route into the Powder River area where the Sioux had been forced to relocate. The whites were eager to build forts along the Bozeman Trail, and they wouldn't take no for an answer.

Once again, the soldiers negotiated peace with the Indians but simultaneously made plans to do whatever they wanted. Colonel Henry Carrington was sent into the Powder River area to begin building forts along the trail at the same time peace talks were being held at Fort Laramie. When a Brulé named Standing Elk went to Fort Laramie and told the Indians what was happening, they grew angry. Red Cloud was among them.

Once gold was discovered in Montana, white soldiers were eager to secure a safe route into the Powder River area.

*Colonel Henry
Carrington*

"The Great Father (president) sends us presents and talks about buying a new road while the soldier chief comes to steal it before the Indian can say yes or no!" Red Cloud cried.

He immediately left the peace talks. Colonel Carrington's men would soon have trouble on their hands.

Meanwhile, Crazy Horse was causing trouble of his own. He was spending a great deal of time with Black Buffalo Woman, who now had three children with her husband No Water. Gossip spread throughout the camp about their relationship, but Crazy Horse didn't care—even though he was a shirt-wearer and was supposed to set an example for others. No Water didn't like the attention Crazy Horse paid to his wife, but he didn't tell him to go away.

Still, Crazy Horse didn't let his time with Black Buffalo Woman interfere with his duties as a warrior. On December 21, 1866, he again served as a decoy in an important battle that came to be known as the Fetterman Massacre.

The Sioux and the Cheyenne were angry about the forts popping up along the Bozeman Trail, especially Fort Phil Kearny. At the foot of the Bighorn Mountains in Powder River country, this fort, along with Fort C. F. Smith and Fort Reno, protected white travelers on the trail. But these forts posed a great threat to the Sioux. This was the last of their buffalo-hunting grounds in the Powder River area, and the Sioux's way of life was jeopardized. About 1,000 Indians called this area their home. If the whites destroyed the land and wildlife as they'd done on the Holy Road, the Sioux would not survive. And they weren't going to disappear without a fight.

The Bozeman Trail was named for adventurer John Bozeman, who founded the passageway in the 1860s. Miners used this route to get to Montana and Idaho in their search for gold. The Bozeman Trail stretched 600 miles (960 km) from Fort Laramie, Wyoming, to present-day Virginia City, Montana.

The Powder River area proved to be one of the most hotly contested regions in the war between whites and Indians. Throughout most of 1866, Crazy Horse and others caused whatever trouble they could, hoping that the whites would leave. All along the Bozeman Trail, they raided wagon trains and Army wagons and attacked prospectors and other travelers.

During the Fetterman Massacre, Crazy Horse, American Horse, He Dog, and other decoys lured

The Powder River area was a valuable hunting ground for the Sioux.

soldiers from Fort Phil Kearny and started shooting at them. As bullets flew, the decoys pretended to be afraid and headed toward a nearby slope called Lodge Trail Ridge. For his part, Crazy Horse pretended his horse was lame. He kept jumping off as if the animal could no longer carry him. He hoped to lure the soldiers closer by making them believe he wouldn't be able to ride away on his horse or attack them by quickly riding toward them. The soldiers fell for this trap and followed the decoys. Leading the way was Captain William J. Fetterman.

An arrogant man, Fetterman once bragged he could destroy the entire Sioux nation with just 80 soldiers. When a group of woodcutters said they were being harassed by Indians, Captain Fetterman demanded that Colonel Carrington let him come to their aid. Carrington reluctantly agreed to let Fetterman and his troops go after the Indians but warned them not to cross over Lodge Trail Ridge. Once past the ridge, the soldiers would be out of sight of the fort.

Sioux Indians sheltered themselves from harsh winter weather on the Plains by moving their camps to wooded areas that blocked the wind. Robes made from buffalo hides also provided protection from the elements.

But the temptation proved too much for Fetterman. He and his men scaled the ridge and were greeted by 2,000 Indians. Fetterman tried to turn back, but it was too late. The soldiers, who were on foot, fell under the weight of the war clubs and the stamping hooves of the Indians' horses.

Captain Fetterman and his men fought for their lives, firing their guns for as long as they could. Crazy Horse and others dragged injured Indian warriors to safety. The blood that dripped from their wounds immediately froze in the frigid winter weather.

The white soldiers' breath came out in cold, smoky plumes as they tried to take a higher position

65

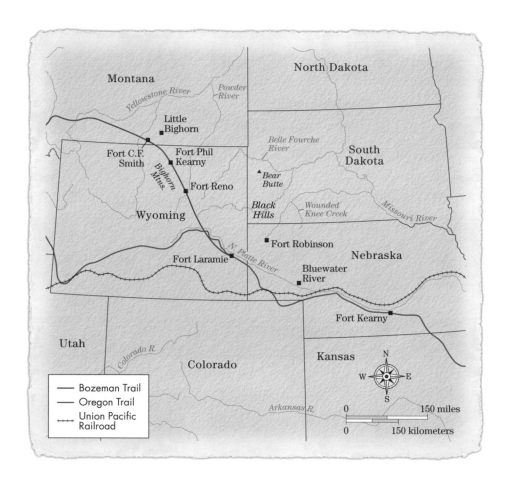

North Dakota

Montana

Yellowstone River

Powder River

Little Bighorn

Belle Fourche River

South Dakota

Fort C.F. Smith

Fort Phil Kearny

Bighorn Mtns.

Fort Reno

Bear Butte

Wyoming

Black Hills

Wounded Knee Creek

Missouri River

Fort Robinson

Fort Laramie

N. Platte River

Nebraska

Bluewater River

Fort Kearny

Utah

Colorado R.

Colorado

Kansas

N
W   E
S

Bozeman Trail
Oregon Trail
Union Pacific Railroad

Arkansas R.

0   150 miles

0   150 kilometers

By the middle to late 1800s, Americans had established various forts and trails leading into the West.

on the slope. The Indian warriors' horses couldn't make the steep, icy climb upward, so the riders dismounted and crawled up the ridge. With bows and arrows at the ready, the Sioux killed all the U.S. troops in less than half an hour.

After collecting all the guns and ammunition they could find, the Indians made carriers for their wounded and left. By the look of the sky, a storm was quickly approaching. More importantly, they didn't want to face the new stream of soldiers that was coming from Fort Phil Kearny. By this time, the Sioux had already lost 13 men.

Before departing, Crazy Horse and Hump searched for their friend Lone Bear. They found him face down in a pile of brush. Still alive, Lone Bear's face and hands were frozen white. He had suffered a gunshot wound to the chest. Lone Bear opened his

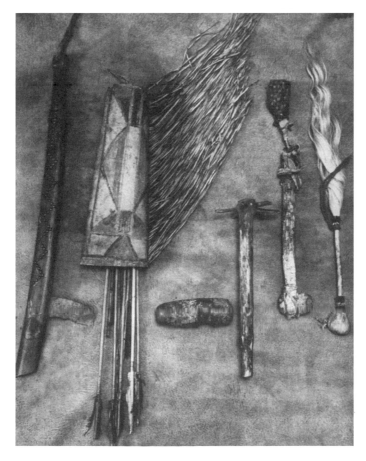

The Sioux used war clubs to fight Fetterman and his soldiers.

Crazy Horse participated in the Wagon Box Fight in the summer of 1867.

eyes as Crazy Horse lifted him from the cold ground. Tears flowed down Hump's face as Lone Bear died in Crazy Horse's arms.

Angry at the death of yet another friend, Crazy Horse was happy to continue causing trouble for whites he believed had invaded his land. Other Indians felt the same way. On August 2, 1867, the two groups clashed in the Wagon Box Fight.

The Indians' targets were woodcutters, working about 5 miles (8 km) west of Fort Phil Kearny. To help protect the men from Indian raids, wagon boxes circled the area where they worked, and 32

soldiers stood guard. Crazy Horse and other warriors attacked the soldiers, believing the whites
would eventually run out of ammunition. At that
point, the Indians planned to scale the wagon boxes
and kill them. But to the Indians' surprise, the soldiers were still firing after three hours of fighting.
With six warriors killed and just as many injured, the
Indians left in defeat.

"We are butchered like the spotted buffalo without ammu-nition!" Crazy Horse cried out in frustration.

Things improved for Crazy Horse and his people in 1868. Another peace treaty found its way to Fort Laramie. Crazy Horse had witnessed many failed treaties, but this one seemed different. All of present-day South Dakota west of the Missouri River would serve as a reservation for the Sioux. This included the Sioux holy lands— the Black Hills. The soldiers agreed to abandon the three forts along the Bozeman Trail, and the Indians would be free to hunt in the Powder River area. It

In 1862, Congress approved the Pacific Railroad Act. The act called for a railroad line that would reach all the way across the country. The Union Pacific expanded west-ward across Nebraska. The Central Pacific extended eastward from California. The two sets of track met on May 10, 1869, in Promontory, Utah, completing a railroad line that stretched from the East Coast to the West Coast. It made the cost of traveling cross-country a lot cheaper, and it saved time.

was determined that this area included land that stretched from west of the Black Hills to the Bighorn Mountains. The North Platte River would serve as the area's southern boundary. At the time

A marker near modern-day Story, Wyoming, where the Wagon Box Fight occurred more than 135 years ago

the treaty was established, no northern boundary was discussed.

In return, the Sioux agreed to allow the completion of the Union Pacific Railroad across Nebraska. In addition, when all the buffalo disappeared, the Sioux would give up their nomadic lifestyle and live in houses, just as the whites did. They would farm on their reservation and educate their children in American schools.

In November 1868, Red Cloud signed the treaty—but only after the forts had been abandoned. To ensure that no one would use the forts, Crazy Horse and his friends set fire to them. Red Cloud promised he would never fight again, and he kept his word. But he warned that he couldn't speak for other Indians.

Crazy Horse was once more free to roam and hunt as he pleased. ॐ

9 BIG BATTLES WITH WHITES AND FAMILY

The summer of 1870 brought more trouble for Crazy Horse. It started when he found himself camped near Black Buffalo Woman on the banks of the Yellowstone River.

Their close friendship had never disappeared as the years passed. In fact, they grew closer. That summer, Crazy Horse gathered a small war party to ride northwest against the Crow, and Black Buffalo Woman chose to be part of it. Leaving her three children with relatives, she rode off with Crazy Horse.

As the pair left camp, people noticed. Everyone knew they were in love. Crazy Horse often looked at Black Buffalo Woman, and his face softened to reveal his feelings. She was beautiful in her plain buckskin.

By 1870, Crazy Horse and Black Buffalo Woman were camped near one another along the Yellowstone River.

Crazy Horse was also quite striking in appearance. His hair was braided and wrapped in beaver fur. Looking much like the horseman in the vision he once had, he wore dark blue leggings and a white buckskin shirt. A single feather lay flat on the back of his head.

When No Water discovered his wife had left with Crazy Horse, his heart filled with rage. He raced after them, armed with a pistol he had borrowed from a friend.

On the second night of their trip, Black Buffalo Woman and Crazy Horse were feasting with friends when the flap of the lodge flew open. No Water stood in the doorway and aimed the pistol at Crazy Horse. In a heartbeat, a bright flash stung Crazy Horse's eyes. A bullet ripped through his upper jaw, and Crazy Horse fell into the fire. As quickly as he appeared, No Water vanished. Black Buffalo Woman also fled, slipping out the back of the lodge.

According to Sioux custom, women were allowed to divorce husbands who no longer pleased them. To get a divorce, a woman simply had to place her husband's belongings outside their lodge. Black Buffalo Woman never did this. Crazy Horse also could have offered her husband No Water horses or other gifts in exchange for marrying Black Buffalo Woman. But in all likelihood, No Water would have refused the trade.

No Water thought he'd killed Crazy Horse. The warrior recovered but was unable to talk for some time because of the damage the bullet had caused. Using hand signals, Crazy Horse made it clear that he wouldn't permit No Water or Black Buffalo Woman to be punished.

No Water apologized by sending two of his best horses to Worm a few days after the attack.

To apologize for his attack on Crazy Horse, No Water offered two of his best horses to Worm.

Eventually, Black Buffalo Woman went back to No Water, and Crazy Horse rejoined his own family. But the memory of the shooting would remain with him forever.

Once Crazy Horse recovered, he was soon forced to deal with more bad news. While he had been off with Black Buffalo Woman, miners had killed his brother, Little Hawk. Crazy Horse felt tremendous guilt because he believed this never would have happened if he hadn't left camp.

Crazy Horse's trip with Black Buffalo Woman also cost him his position as a shirt-wearer. He had put selfish interests before the good of the tribe. As his prized shirt was carried away, Crazy Horse felt sadness but no anger. He knew he had brought the punishment on himself.

"When we were made (shirt wearers), we were bound by very strict rules as to what we should do and what not to do, which were very hard for us to follow," Crazy Horse's friend He Dog said. He had been made a shirt-wearer in a later ceremony. "I have always kept the oaths I made then, but Crazy Horse did not. The shirt (belonging to Crazy Horse) was never given to anyone else."

Eventually, No Water took Black Buffalo Woman and their children to live on a reservation. But news of another child born to Black Buffalo Woman did reach the Sioux. It was said the baby girl had noticeably light skin and hair.

"Many people believe this child was Crazy Horse's daughter, but it was never known for certain," said He Dog.

After marrying, a Sioux couple usually moved into the wife's home, where the roles of husband and wife were clearly defined. The man was responsible for providing food for the family and protecting them from enemies. The woman ruled over the home and family. When children came along, they became the center of attention for the Sioux family, and their parents helped them learn their duties to the tribe.

Those who loved Crazy Horse saw the whole incident as proof that he needed to find his own wife. In 1871, he came home from a hunting trip to find a woman named Black Shawl waiting for him. They had much in common. Both were quiet and nearly 30, but Crazy Horse wanted to make sure she knew what she was getting into by marrying him. Crazy Horse went to his stepmother and asked her to have a talk with Black Shawl.

"You must say there will be little joy in a life with me." Crazy Horse didn't sing, dance, or even talk much, and he worried this would bring sadness to anyone who married him.

"The Black Shawl knows these things," his stepmother said. "She is also a quiet-mouth one."

"Tell her she will choose a man who is as a dead one, for I have now no wish to live," Crazy Horse insisted.

As Crazy Horse had requested, his stepmother spoke with Black Shawl. She returned with a beautiful pair of moccasins that were beaded with lightning

bolts and placed them in front of Crazy Horse. This made it official—Crazy Horse and Black Shawl were married.

"All I can say about that is that both Crazy Horse and my sister stayed single much longer than is usual among our people," Black Shawl's brother Red Feather said.

Despite his concerns, Crazy Horse grew to love Black Shawl. And in the fall of 1871, joy came into their lives when a daughter was born. Black Shawl worried that Crazy Horse would be disappointed their baby wasn't a son, but Crazy Horse couldn't have loved her more. Crazy Horse declared:

> *Then it is a daughter, a new daughter for the Oglalas, and she shall grow up a great mother of the people, and everybody shall stand in wonder before her sacred ways and she shall be called They Are Afraid of Her.*

Sadly, their joy would be short-lived. White travelers had brought diseases such as tuberculosis, cholera, and smallpox to Indian lands. Black Shawl caught tuberculosis and survived. It is believed that They Are Afraid of Her developed cholera, but she was too young to fight the disease. She died when she was about 3 years old. Crazy Horse mourned his beloved daughter's death.

At about the same time, gold was discovered in the Black Hills. According to the treaty formed in 1868, whites weren't allowed in this area, but that didn't stop them from pouring in. When Lieutenant Colonel George Armstrong Custer learned of the

George
Armstrong
Custer

gold, he had a scout travel to Fort Laramie to send a telegram announcing the discovery. Once the news broke, miners quickly found their way into the Dakota Territory to seek their fortunes.

Officials in Washington, D.C., tried to get the Indians to sell the Black Hills. Crazy Horse and Hunkpapa Sioux chief Sitting Bull were against the

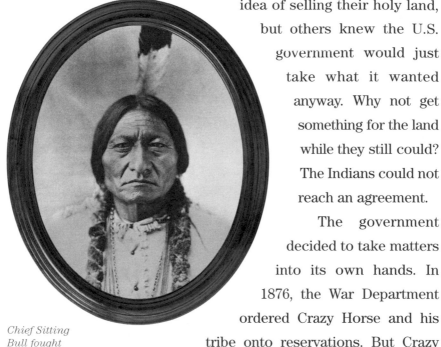

Chief Sitting Bull fought Custer in the Battle of the Little Bighorn.

idea of selling their holy land, but others knew the U.S. government would just take what it wanted anyway. Why not get something for the land while they still could? The Indians could not reach an agreement.

The government decided to take matters into its own hands. In 1876, the War Department ordered Crazy Horse and his tribe onto reservations. But Crazy Horse, Sitting Bull, and their people refused to be corralled. They would fight to remain free.

On June 17, 1876, General George Crook advanced up Rosebud Creek in an effort to attack Sitting Bull's people on the Little Bighorn River. But the general never reached his destination. Crazy Horse rounded up about 1,200 Sioux and Cheyenne to fend off Crook and his men. Though Crook's troops numbered nearly 1,000, they were spread out on both sides of the river. Crazy Horse and his warriors bravely charged at the soldiers. Hand-to-hand combat continued throughout the day. By evening, Crook and his troops had given up.

Both sides lost many men, but the Indians claimed victory because they had prevented the soldiers from reaching the Little Bighorn.

On June 25, barely a week later, Crazy Horse joined Sitting Bull in fighting Custer and his 7th Cavalry in the Battle of the Little Bighorn. Custer's scouts warned him they had never seen such a large gathering of Indians. They predicted that many U.S. soldiers would die if Custer attacked.

Ignoring the advice of his scouts and offers of extra troops and weapons, Custer pushed on. Leading 647 men, he attacked a village of about 9,000 Indians along the banks of the Little Bighorn River. Custer had forced his troops to march through the night to reach their destination. The men were so tired and so outnumbered that they didn't stand a chance. But Custer was seeking glory and was certain he would find it in this battle.

Crazy Horse and Sitting Bull launched a counterattack, hitting the soldiers from the north and west. Warriors following

A few weeks before the Battle of the Little Bighorn, Sitting Bull performed a sacred Sun Dance. As was customary in the ceremony, he pierced his skin with sharp bones to show how much he was willing to sacrifice for his people. In his pain, Sitting Bull had a grand vision of American soldiers falling from the sky. He believed that the dead soldiers meant that the Sioux would soon win a great battle. Just weeks later, his vision came true.

The Indians emerged victorious from the Battle of the Little Bighorn.

Hunkpapa chief Gall hit the whites from the south and east. The Indians noticed how the legs of the white men shook with weariness and observed how many found it difficult to even raise their guns. In a strategic error that would prove deadly,

Custer had divided his troops into three small groups. In less than an hour, Custer and his 200 soldiers lay dead. More than 60 other soldiers would also die.

Hunkpapa warrior Bad Soup pointed out Custer's body to a friend after the battle.

"There he lies," Bad Soup said. "He thought he was going to be the greatest man in the world. But there he is."

In the end, however, the great victory at the Little Bighorn bought the Sioux little time. General Nelson A. Miles battled the Indians well into the winter months. The constant harassment from soldiers, the decline of the buffalo, and the suffering of his people finally led Crazy Horse to surrender on May 6, 1877. ✑

George Armstrong Custer was well known among the Indians, but they probably didn't recognize him during the Battle of the Little Bighorn. He'd cut his famous, flowing red hair before the fighting began.

10 A TRAGIC FATE AT FORT ROBINSON

Chapter

c⌒x⌒⊃

At Fort Robinson in northwest Nebraska, Crazy Horse turned over his rifle and horses to the white officers.

Before his surrender, he negotiated an agreement with General Crook. Among other things, Crook assured Crazy Horse that he would get his own reservation in the Powder River area, and that his people would be able to leave the reservation on 40-day buffalo hunts. Ultimately, both of these promises were broken.

At first, Crazy Horse and his people found a home with Red Cloud. In the end, however, this arrangement made Crazy Horse miserable. Red Cloud and others were jealous of him because he still carried himself like a warrior. He reminded the

Red Cloud (1821?–1909) was was a leader of the Oglalas.

The surrender of
Crazy Horse was
such a big event that
the New York Times
reported it in its
May 8, 1877, issue.

Indians of the proud people they had once been. Crazy Horse hadn't been defeated. He had surrendered because he felt it was the right thing to do for his tribe. Adding to this tension was the fact that many of the white officers respected Crazy Horse. Rumors spread that they were going to name him chief of all the Sioux.

In truth, the soldiers weren't sure what to do with Crazy Horse. Some said he should be left alone and given time to adjust to his new life. Others didn't trust him and feared he would stir rebellion. A few even suggested he be imprisoned in Florida.

But before anything could come to pass, the Nez Perce Indians started their 1,300-mile (2,092-km) march through Idaho, Wyoming, and Montana. They had been granted a reservation in Washington and Oregon territories in 1855, but when gold was discovered on the reservation, the size of their homeland shrank. When their land was opened to white settlers in the 1870s, the Nez Perce were given 30 days to move to a different reservation in Idaho. Their leader, Chief Joseph, advised his people to obey, but trouble erupted when members of the tribe killed four white men. Fearing the consequences of this killing, the Nez Perce fled toward Canada.

During the 1870s, the U.S. government ordered the Nez Perce to move to a reservation in Idaho.

Crook was responsible for making sure the Nez Perce didn't reach their destination. Lieutenant Philo Clark suggested asking Crazy Horse and his people to help stop the flight of the Nez Perce. Crook talked to Crazy Horse, but the warrior didn't understand. When he surrendered, Crazy Horse had been forced to give up his weapons and was made to promise that he would never fight again. Now the white men wanted him to do just the opposite. But despite the soldiers' mixed messages, Crazy Horse eventually agreed to the plan.

We came in for peace. We are tired of war and talking of war," Crazy Horse said. "From back when Conquering Bear was still with us we have been lied to and fooled by the whites, and here it is the same, but still we want to do what is asked of us and if the Great Father wants us to fight we will go north and fight until not a Nez Perce is left.

Unfortunately, the interpreter, a scout named Frank Grouard, told Crook that Crazy Horse said he would fight until the last white person was dead. As a result of the misunderstanding, Crazy Horse was never involved in the capture of the Nez Perce.

In September 1877, Crazy Horse left the reservation without permission. He took Black Shawl, still suffering from tuberculosis, to see her parents. In Crazy Horse's absence, Woman's Dress met with Crook. During this meeting, he lied and told Crook that Crazy Horse planned to kill him.

Crook believed Woman's Dress and immediately called for Crazy Horse's arrest. A large group of soldiers and Indians—including No Water—captured him. Nearly 1,000 Indians participated in or witnessed his arrest. Crazy Horse was confused. He'd done so much for his people throughout the years. Why were they treating him this way?

On September 6, 1877, Crazy Horse was returned to Fort Robinson. Accompanied by Indian

agent Jesse Lee, Crazy Horse believed he would be allowed to speak with the fort's commander, Colonel Luther Bradley, to straighten out any confusion. But Bradley never intended to meet with him. He ordered that Crazy Horse be jailed in the fort until he could be sent to a prison in Florida.

As Crazy Horse approached the filthy cells where other Indians sat in chains, he knew he was in trouble. He tried to break free and run away, but Little Big Man—an old friend who now served as an Indian policeman—jumped on his back and tried to hold his arms. It was just like what had happened to the horseman in Crazy Horse's vision!

Crazy Horse managed to free one arm and grab a knife that was hidden under the blanket he was wearing. He injured Little Big Man, but other Indians struggled to get the flailing warrior under control. In the chaos, a soldier named William Gentles rushed forward and stabbed Crazy Horse in the back with a bayonet. The famous warrior sunk to the dusty ground, mortally wounded.

After much discussion about how the Indians would react to Crazy Horse's impending death, the white officers decided to move the dying man into an office. They tried to place him on a cot, but Crazy Horse refused and asked to be put on the floor instead. He preferred to spend his last moments on the bare earth, instead of a white man's bed. With Worm at his side, he died. He was about 37 years old.

Crazy Horse's body was placed on a burial scaffold outside the fort. When the U.S. government moved the Sioux north to the Missouri River area, they took the body with them. No one knows for sure where Crazy Horse was finally buried, but leg-

A drawing of Crazy Horse's death by Amos Bad Heart Bull, a member of the Oglala Sioux tribe

end says it was near Wounded Knee Creek in present-day South Dakota.

Today, an image of Crazy Horse is being carved on Thunderhead Mountain in South Dakota's Black Hills. In 1939, Lakota chief Henry Standing Bear asked artist Korczak Ziolkowski to sculpt Crazy Horse's likeness above the land the deceased leader loved. The largest sculpture in the world, the Crazy Horse Memorial is located 17 miles (27 km)

A likeness of Crazy Horse's face is carved into Thunderhead Mountain. The massive project is funded through private gifts.

southwest of Mount Rushmore. It's not far from Custer, South Dakota—a town named after George Armstrong Custer, Crazy Horse's enemy.

"My fellow chiefs and I would like the white man to know the red man has great heroes, too," Standing Bear said.

When it is finished, the carving will be 563 feet

(172 m) tall and 641 (195 m) feet long. The scene shows Crazy Horse, sitting tall and strong, his left arm outstretched and pointing over the top of his horse's head. Ziolkowski explained that his carving depicts the warrior answering a white man who cruelly asked, "Where are your lands now?" Crazy Horse proudly replied, "My lands are where my dead lie buried."

Mount Rushmore is another mountain carving, but it includes the faces of four U.S. presidents—George Washington, Thomas Jefferson, Theodore Roosevelt, and Abraham Lincoln. At its tallest point, the sculpture reaches about 60 feet (18 m).

Ziolkowski worked on the massive monument until his death in 1982. His family continues to help make his dream a reality. Through the years, more than 8 million tons of rock have been removed as the image has taken shape.

In June 1998, the face on the carving was dedicated. On a cold, wet day, about 7,000 people braved the elements and watched the ceremony. The crowd included individuals from a wide variety of backgrounds, but all attended to honor Crazy Horse—a man of courage who always remembered to look after the needs of the less fortunate.

CRAZY HORSE'S LIFE

1840?

Born near Bear Butte, close to present-day Sturgis, South Dakota

1844

Mother, Rattle Blanket Woman, dies

1840   1850

1848

The Communist Manifesto by German writer Karl Marx is widely distributed

1846

Irish potato famine reaches its worst

WORLD EVENTS

1854
Leaves camp after the Grattan Massacre and receives a vision of his future

1857
Finally tells his father about his vision

1855
Helps survivors of a massacre at Little Thunder's Bluewater River village

1852
Postage stamps are widely used

1856
Nikola Tesla, electrical engineer and inventor, is born

CRAZY HORSE'S LIFE

1858

Earns the name
Crazy Horse after
displaying courage
on the battlefield

1861

Enjoys a brief period
of peace as the Civil
War draws many sol-
diers on the frontier
forts back East to fight

1860

1858

English scientist
Charles Darwin
presents his theory
of evolution

1860

Austrian composer
Gustav Mahler is
born in Kalischt
(now in Austria)

1862

Victor Hugo publishes
Les Misérables

WORLD EVENTS

1865

Involved in an attack on settlers crossing the Platte River

1866

On December 21, engages in fighting related to the Fetterman Massacre

1867

Participates in the Wagon Box fight near Fort Phil Kearny on August 2

1865

Lewis Carroll writes *Alice's Adventures in Wonderland*

1867

Russia sells Alaska to the United States

CRAZY HORSE'S LIFE

1868

Optimistic that things will improve for his people when the Treaty of 1868 is signed

1870

Leaves with Black Buffalo Woman and is shot by her husband, No Water

1871

Marries Black Shawl, who gives birth to their daughter, They Are Afraid of Her, later that year

1870

1869

The periodic table of elements is invented by Dimitri Mendeleyev

1873

Typewriters get the QWERTY keyboard

WORLD EVENTS

1874

Mourns when his only daughter, They Are Afraid of Her, dies

1876

Fights in the Battle of the Little Bighorn on June 25

1877

Surrenders at Fort Robinson, Nebraska, on May 0, dies there September 6

1877

German inventor Nikolaus A. Otto works on what will become the internal combustion engine for automobiles

1876

Alexander Graham Bell uses the first telephone to speak to his assistant, Thomas Watson

DATE OF BIRTH: Fall 1840?

BIRTHPLACE: Bear Butte, near present-day Sturgis, South Dakota

FATHER: Was named Crazy Horse, but later took the name Worm

MOTHER: Rattle Blanket Woman

EDUCATION: No formal education

SPOUSE: Black Shawl

DATE OF MARRIAGE: 1871

CHILDREN: They Are Afraid of Her (1871–1874)

DATE OF DEATH: September 6, 1877

PLACE OF BURIAL: No one knows for sure, but many believe Crazy Horse was buried in the Pine Ridge area of South Dakota along Wounded Knee Creek

In the Library

Brennan, Kristine. *Crazy Horse*. Philadelphia: Chelsea House Publishers, 2002.

Cunningham, Chet. *Chief Crazy Horse*. Minneapolis: Lerner Publications, 2000.

Freedman, Russell. *The Life and Death of Crazy Horse*. New York: Holiday House, 1996.

Goldman, Martin S. *Crazy Horse: War Chief of the Oglala Sioux*. New York: Franklin Watts, 1996.

Nobleman, Marc Tyler. *The Battle of the Little Bighorn*. Minneapolis: Compass Point Books, 2002.

Razzi, Jim. *Custer and Crazy Horse: A Story of Two Warriors*. New York: Scholastic, 1989.

Look for more Signature Lives
books about this era:

James Beckwourth: *Mountaineer, Scout, and Pioneer*

Geronimo: *Apache Warrior*

Sam Houston: *Texas Hero*

Bridget "Biddy" Mason: *From Slave to Businesswoman*

Sarah Winnemucca: *Scout, Activist, and Teacher*

Zebulon Pike: *Explorer and Soldier*

ON THE WEB

For more information on *Crazy Horse*, use FactHound to track down Web sites related to this book.

1. Go to *www.facthound.com*
2. Type in a search word related to this book or this book ID: 0756509998
3. Click on the *Fetch It* button.

FactHound will find the best Web sites for you.

HISTORIC SITES

Crazy Horse Memorial
Avenue of the Chiefs
Crazy Horse, SD 57730
605/673-4681
To view the mountain carving being created in Crazy Horse's honor

Fort Laramie National Historic Site
965 Gray Rocks Road
Fort Laramie, WY 82212
307/837-2221
To learn about the Great Sioux War

Fort Robinson State Park
Fort Robinson Museum
P.O. Box 304
Crawford, NE 69339-0304
308/665-2919
To visit the spot where Crazy Horse died